Weaving Made Easy

How to Weave for Beginners

Table of Contents

Chapter 1: Weaving Dictionary 6
Chapter 2: What is Weaving?..10
   The 3 Basic Types of Weaving 11
      Twill..11
      Satin Weave 14
      Plain Weave 15

   The Process of Weaving 16
   Other Loom Motions..17
      Secondary Loom Motion 18
      Tertiary Loom Motions...18

   Materials for Weaving..18
Chapter 3: Weaving Patterns, Tips, Tricks, and How To
....21
   Coasters 21
   Weaving On Rectangular Cardboards 26
   Weaving Using Pins 31
   Wheels and Hoops as Looms 35
   Using the Weave-It Loom..40
Conclusion...45

Chapter 1: Weaving Dictionary

Before we start learning what is weaving and tackling a brief history of weaving, we first need to know the meanings of various weaving jargons. This way, once we begin learning how to we weave, it is easier for us to understand the meaning of the words used and the context.

Beat – this is the act of pressing the yarn with a rigid heddle in place. Commonly a heddle is used in tandem with a loom. But, there are DIY cases were a loom is not used and so is a heddle. Sometimes in lieu of a heddle, a comb is used.

Beater – then the beater is the instrument used to press the wefts together to keep the rows compact.

Cross – a cross is formed at one or both ends of the warp in order to keep the yarns organized.

Dent – a dent is a single space in a reed. As an example, weavers use dent like "8-dent rigid heddle," this simply means that it has 8-spaces in an inch.

Draft – this is a chart that instructs the weaver on how to treadle a pattern, tie up shafts, and thread the heddle. This is usually used for a table or floor loom.

Ends per Inch (EPI) – this is the number of yarns in an inch of warp.

Fell – This is where the last laid weft pick is pressed into place. Commonly, the fell line advances as the weaving advances.

Float – This is a weft or warp yarn that travels over more than one weft pick or warp end.

Header – this is a waste yarn woven at the start of the project in order to spread the warp to its full width thereby providing an even and firm surface to begin your weaving.

Heddle – this is the molded plastic piece in the rigid-heddle that forms to the holes between the slots. When speaking of shaft looms, heddles are made of string or metal and move freely on a frame shaft. The rigid-heddle got its name from the fact that heddles are commonly held rigidly in place.

Pick and End – one weft thread is called a Pick. One warp thread is called an end.

Picks per inch (PPI) – in an inch of weaving, these are the number of weft yarns.

Reed – this is term used in shaft loom. It commonly refers to a part that is like a rigid heddle but it does not have holes. It presses the yarn into place, maintains the warp width, and determines the sett of the cloth. Unlike the rigid heddle, it cannot shed. Sometimes, you may hear or read weavers referring to the rigid-heddle as reed because these two share the same functions.

Rigid-heddle – This is a part of a loom that is made up of molded plastic forms held by two wooden supports rigidly in order to form a hole or a slot configuration.

Selvedge – the edge of a wooden cloth. There's also selvage which is the closely woven space along the edge of cloth.

Sett – In the rigid-heddle, these are the spacing of the warp yarns.

Shed – This is the space created when the rigid-heddle is lowered or lifted. You can also think of this spot as the place that shelters the weft.

Shot – one pass of the weft through the shed.

Shuttle – this is known as the weaver's needle. Generally, this can be just a piece of wood where the weft is wrapped. If the yarn fits, shuttle can also take the form of bobby hairpins, bodkins, tapestry needles, or the fingers.

Take-up – take-up is caused by two actions. The first being, the weft does not travel in a straight line, instead it bends under and over the warp. The second is, once the woven cloth is removed from the loom's tension, it rebounds. Due to these two phenomena, you need to factor in extra weft yardage and warp length when weaving so that you ensure that the end product is the size you want it to be.

Warp – these are the yarns held taut on the loom.

Chapter 2: What is Weaving?

Weaving is one way of producing textile from two different sets of yarns. These yarns are interlaced at right angles in order to make a cloth or fabric. Weaving is nearly the same as plaiting, braiding, felting, and knitting.

The longitudinal or vertical yarns are called the warp and the latitudinal or horizontal yarns are known as the filling or weft. Weft is an old English term that means "that which is woven;" another old English term for it is woof.

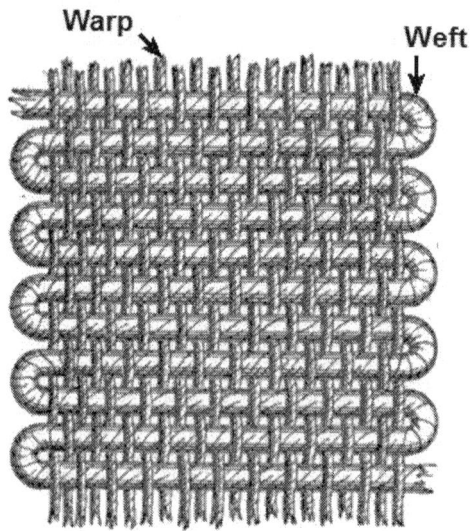

When you weave a cloth, you usually do this on a loom. A loom is a device that holds the warp yarn in place as the weaver weaves in and out the filling yarn. But, weaving can also be done without the use of a loom like back-strap, tablet weaving, and other techniques without looms.

The 3 Basic Types of Weaving

The method of the weft and the warp threads interlace with each other is known as the weave. Basically, there are three basic types of weave and they are:

Twill

Twill is a type of weaving pattern with a diagonal parallel ribs, compared to plain and satin weave. This is usually done by passing a weft thread over one or more warp threads and then under two or more warp threads and so on, creating a pattern. Before beginning the next shot, a "step" or offset is applied in order to create the characteristic diagonal pattern. Due to the characteristic of twill weave pattern, it drapes well. Here are some examples of twill weave pattern:

Herringbone

Diamond Twill

Structure and Characteristics

In a twill weave, each filling or weft yarn floats across the warp yarns in a progression of interlacings to the right or left such that it creates a distinct diagonal line. This diagonal line is referred to as a wale. The term float is used to refer to the portion of a yarn that crosses over two or more yarns from the opposite direction.

When it comes to twill weave patterns, it is usually denoted as a fraction. For example, 2/2 wherein the numerator indicates the number of warp yarns that the weft must go over and the denominator shows the number of warp yarns that the weft must go under. Please look at the photo below:

The step or offset created the wale or the diagonal line characteristic of a twill weave pattern. Further, the 2/2 pattern is read as "2 up, 2 down).

Commonly, a twill pattern cloth has a back and front side. It is not like a plain weave where the front and back looks the same. The front side of the twill pattern fabric is called as the technical face and technical back is for the back. The technical face of the twill pattern weave has a more pronounced wale. The technical face is more attractive and durable.

Twill cloths stain and soil less due to its uneven surface compared to its plain weave counterpart. Sheer fabrics are seldom made with a twill weave. Denims are a good example of twill. Since twill cloths soil and stain less this is a common fabric used for durable upholstery and work clothes.

Satin Weave

A satin weave cloth characteristically has a dull back and glossy surface. It is commonly featured with a four or more weft or fill yarns floating over a warp yarn. These floats give satin its even sheen, compared with other type of weaves where the light is scattered a lot by the fibres. With satin, it has fewer tucks and more floats so light is not scattered as much.

Since a satin fabric have higher luster because of the higher number of floats in the cloth it is a typical cloth used in beddings. Further, it is also widely used in apparel like neckties, shirts, briefs, boxers, evening gowns, blouses, night gowns and many more.

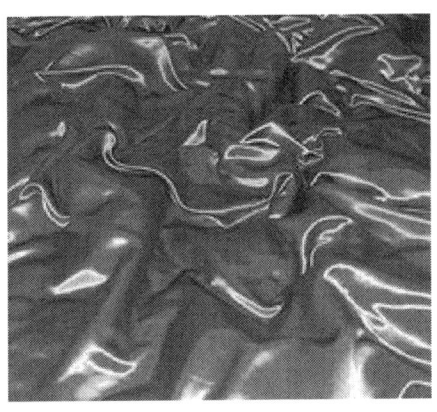

Plain Weave

Plain weave is also known in many names like taffeta weave, linen weave, and tabby weave. It is the most basic of the three fundamental types of weave patterns. It is hard wearing and strong that's why it is a well-loved fabric used in furnishings and fashion.

In plain weave, the weft and the warp are aligned in such a way that they create a simple crisscross pattern. Each weft thread goes up and then goes down a warp yarn in alternating fashion. Then, in the next shot the weft thread begins in the opposite manner, so if the weft above it over the warp yarn, then in the next shot the weft begins under the warp yarn, then goes up, and so on and so forth. Please see the picture below for a better idea.

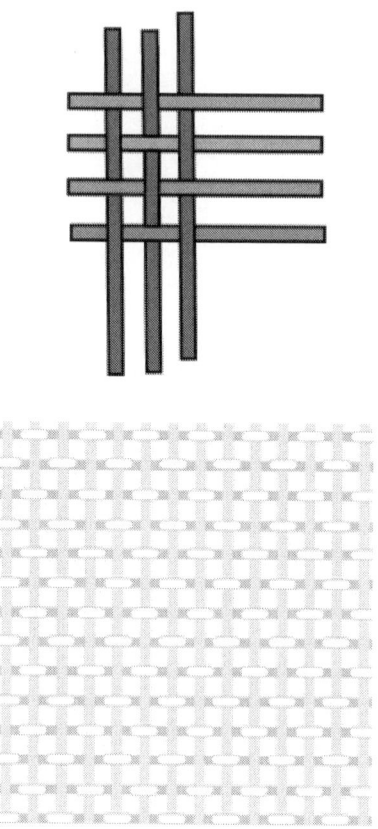

The Process of Weaving

Basically in weaving, it only involves 3 processes given that you are using a loom. When it comes to using other non-loom weaving techniques, they also basically make use of the same technique, however the instruments or equipment use may differ in name and structure but they basically share the same function. So, the three basic processes are as follows:

1) Shedding – This is the process wherein the ends are separated with the up and down movement of the heddle to form the shed or the space where the pick can pass. The pick is the weft thread that needs to be threaded over and under the warp yarn.
2) Picking – this is the process of interlacing the pick or weft over and under the warp yarn. This is how you advance your cloth by adding another shot. Commonly the pick is propelled across the loom by shuttle, rapier, air-jet, or by hand.
3) Beating – this is the process by which the weft is pushed up against the fell of the cloth by the reed or beater.

Other Loom Motions

Aside from the basic movements of the loom as detailed above, there are also other motions and they are as follows:

Secondary Loom Motion

- Take Up Motion – this takes up the woven cloth in a determined manner so that you can maintain the density of the filling.
- Let Off Motion – this is the movement wherein the warp is let off the warp beam at a regulated speed in order to make the filling of the required and even design.

Tertiary Loom Motions

The tertiary motions are related to stop movements and they are: the weft stop motion and the warp stop motion. These stop movements are used in the event of a thread break.

Materials for Weaving

The traditional threads are linen, cotton, and wool, when it comes to weaving. However, there are also unconventional items that can be used to make your weaving prettier and more unique. So, here are a list of great threads you can use and its corresponding looms.

- Novelty Looms – Metallic papers, cotton tape, crepe paper raffia, raffia, cellophane lampshade winding, lace insertion, passe partout, and ribbon.

- Loom with Heddles or Shuttle Weaving – the best material to use is linen or cotton warp—carpet thread or string is also a good alternative. Wool is more like to fuzz and interfere with the heddles function. For the weft, cotton yarns, loosely woven braids, and wool yarn.

- Simple Frame Loom – hemp twine is great as a warp. For weft, yarns can be used whild rags are also recommended because they bulk up well.

- Adjustable Hand Loom – Old stockings, rag strips, ribbon tubing, cellophane ribbon preferably twisted by hand, crepe paper raffia, raffia, cord, and heavy yarns.

- "Weave-It" Loom – For chair backs, bureau scarves, bedspreads, and luncheon sets: cotton and linen floss. For bags, dresses, and sweaters: crepe boucle, wool, tweed yarns, Shetland, and Germantown. For baby sweaters, coats, and blankets: Germantown worsted and Shetland floss. For Afghans: scotch sport yarns, knitting worsted, and Germantown Zephyr.

- Wheels – All sorts of yarns, knitted underwear cut into strips and dyed, old silk stockings, bias binding cotton tape, and rags of silk, cotton, and wool.

- Cardboard rectangles and circles – bias binding cotton tape, carpet thread, linen thread, cotton thread, wool thread, loosely woven braids, soutache braid, narrow cellophane ribbon, crepe paper raffia, raffia, and colored string.

Chapter 3: Weaving Patterns, Tips, Tricks, and How To

In this chapter, we will be learning how to weave using various weaving tools that are appropriate for beginners like you.

Coasters

Coasters are a great project to make as a beginner because they are small and useful. It is also quite visible when you entertain visitors. It adds a nice touch to your home and you can easily showcase your coaster work to your friends and family. This type of weaving can also be used to create cuffs, collars, belts, and doilies. So, once you get the hang of it, you can exand your expertise by creating diverse patterns.

Materials:
Heavy cardboard
Pencil
Ruler
Scissors
1 yard Warp thread (soft cord) 1/16-inch thick
5 yards Weft thread
Shuttle

Directions:

1) Making the loom: Begin by making the loom. To do this, cut a circle with a 3.5-inch diameter. Then with a ruler and pencil, evenly divide the circle into half, then in quarters, and then in eights, until you have evenly divided the circle into 16 equal sections. Then choose a section and divide it into two. Then, cut a V-shape notch at the pencil marks, so that you get a total of 17 notches.

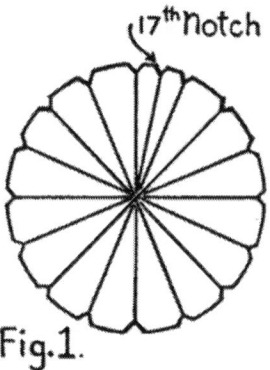

Fig.1.

2) Set Up The Warp Threads. The next stage is setting up the warp threads. Begin by pasting the end of the warp thread in the center of the loom. From the center, bring the warp thread up through a notch, then slide it at the back of the board and out through an adjoining notch

and going straight over the middle of the circle and straight to the other notch, then back of the board and out to the adjoining notch and the process goes on until all notches are filled with warp thread. On the last winding, bring the warp thread back to the center of the circle that means on the last notch, you will have a double strand.

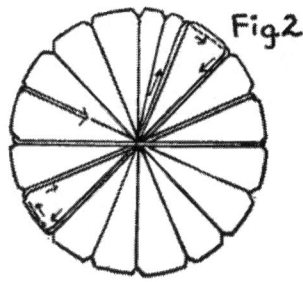

3) Weaving Process. Now that you have setup your loom and your warp thread, you can begin weaving. All you have to do is thread your weft thread into the shuttle and begin weaving from the center of the coaster. Go over one warp thread, and then under, over, under, repeating the process alternatingly. Treat the warp thread with a double strand, just as if it were single stranded. When you reach the second row, on the warp threads you passed under, this tie go over it, and for

the threads you passed over, this tie you go over it. Do the same for the third and succeeding rows until you reach the end of the loom. And do not forget, as you finish each row; push the first rows together tightly. The farther you get from the center, try to release the tension.

4) Continue weaving until the circle is around 2.25-inches in diameter. Cut the cord and join the weft and the warp cord by tying a knot and clipping the ends short. Weave two more rows with the weft cord and the finish with the warp corp. To finish, slip-stitch the cord to the nearest loop. Cut the cord and remove the weaving from the loom by slipping the loops from the notches.

5) Purse Weaving Idea: Using this techniques you can make a purse which needs two circles of woven yarn sewn together. Around half of the circumference, it has a zipper and that handle can be made of thickly braided yarn and sewn at the ends of the purse.

6) Belt Weaving Idea: you can get an idea by checking the photos below. The woven circles on the belt are made from crepe paper raffia using the same process as the coaster.

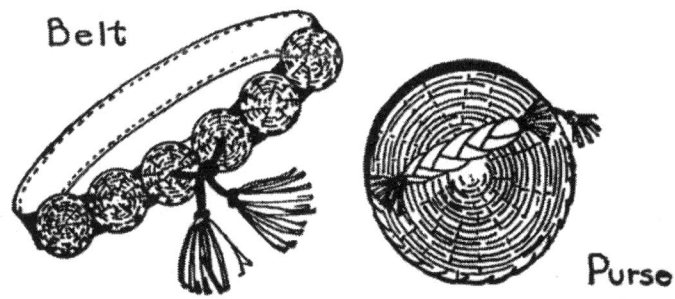

7) Other weaving style: You can also make use of the Spider web weaving style. To do this, cut an EVEN number of notches, pass the needled under each warp thread and make a loop around the thread as shown in diagram.

Weaving On Rectangular Cardboards

Weaving on a rectangular shaped cardboard is easy and you can make a lot of things from it, like a purse. These directions I am about to show you is for a stripe purse. Please feel free to make your own color combination to suit your desires.

Materials:
Stiff cardboard
3 yard brown 3-ply wool
15 yards green 3-ply wool
40 yards tan 3 ply wool
Pencil
Ruler
Scissors

Directions:

1) Make the loom: To begin making the loom, cut a stiff cardboard into 13-inch long by 7.5-inch wide in order to get a finished purse of 6.5 x 4.5 inches. First draw vertical lines, from top to bottom at ¼-inch distance to one another. Then create horizontal lines, from side to side, at ½-inch per line. Then create a mark on all the top and bottom pencil marks, all in all you

will have 27 marks. Notch these 27 marks into a V shape, just like what you did with the coaster loom. You can also check the figure below.

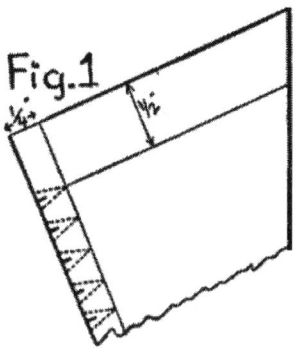

Fig.1

2) Setting Up the Warp Yarn: Now that you have notched your loom, it is ready to be set up with warp threads. Begin at the lower left notch and tie the end of the green yarn to the loom. You can picture this out better by looking at the diagram below. Then bring the yarn all the way across to the other side (horizontally) to the opposite notch, going to the back of the notch and right out the adjacent notch, then going across the board and all the way back (horizontally) to the opposite notch. Then repeat the process until you reach the other end of the loom. And once

you are at the end, just tie the end of the warp thread to the loom.

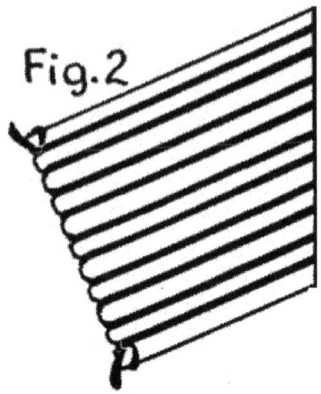

Fig.2

3) Let the Weaving begin! So now that you have the warp threads all set, we are ready to begin weaving. Start with the tan yarn and thread it through a shuttle. Begin at the outer edge of the lower right corner and slip the end of the weft. Then weave back, going to the left, going over and under as you pass each warp thread until you reach the opposite end. Then turn back, weaving over the threads you passed under and weaving under the threads that you passed over in the first line. You can check the figure below to better picture out what we are doing here. So, what you will do is basically start by making the border and they are 7 tan rows, followed by 4 brown rows, 4 tan rows, 5

green rows, 4 tan rows, and 4 brown rows. The remainder of the bag is colored brown.

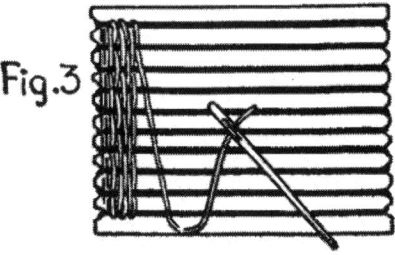

Fig.3

4) On the border, leave a 1-inch end of the color thread when you are done with that specific color. You can just catch this end with a crochet hook to prevent unraveling. Now, if a thread ends in the middle of a row, what you need to do is start the new thread at least 1-inch before the old thread runs out.

5) As much as possible, keep your weaving edges as straight as possible by keeping the weft thread tension uniformly. Ensure that the rows are even. You can remove the weaving from the cardboard by lifting loops from notches.

6) To finish the bag, beginning at the plain end of the bag, line the whole 9-inch length. The flap of the bag is not lined. Then sew up the sides of the bag and add a decorative snap. You can better visualize the project by checking out the figure below.

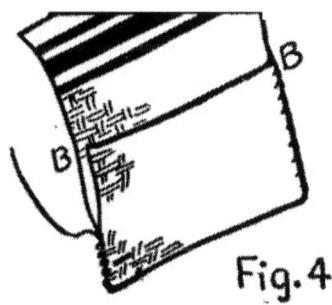
Fig. 4

7) Novel effects: If you are tired of the same old same old, over and under type of weaving, you can create nice visual effects by using wide warp threads and wide weft threads with narrow weft or the same width for warp and weft.

8) With this type of weaving, you can create various items around the house like place mat, bracelet, belt, and even as decorative framed items.

Weaving Using Pins

If you find notches not your thing, then you can make use of pins. The process is just the same, you make use of a thick cardboard, the only difference lies on the fact that this time you are not going to cut the edges of the cardboard into little V-shapes, called notches, because in their place, all you do is push a pin. In this direction, I am going to teach you how to weave an evening bag using pins. Please feel free to vary the colors of the threads.

Materials:
Pins
20 yards white soutache braid
20 yards black soutache braid
Stiff and thick cardboard

Directions:

1) Begin by cutting your board into a 4 ¾-inch square. Place the pins on one side on the board (this will be the top of your loom) at exactly, ½-inch apart—through this, you will have a 1/8-inch margin at each side of the board. All in all, you will have 19 pins setup at the top of the board. You can check the figure below to better visualize this step.

Fig.1

2) Setup your warp thread. To begin setting up your warp thread, begin at the lower left corner of the board. Make sure that your braid is hanging for at least 1 ½ inches (which you will fasten to this corner of the loom with another pin). Wind the thread up and around the first pin at the top of the board, then go back down the bottom of the loom, up the back of the loom and around the top of the first pin (again), and then you go back down, around the board, and back up to the second pin. Repeat this process over and over again until you reach the other end of the loom. Once you have finished looping the thread on the last pin, bring the braid back to the bottom and pin it to the lower right corner, just as you

did when you started. See the figure below for a better understanding.

Fig.2

3) Weaving the weft. Now that you have set up your loom, it is time to start weaving. Now, the weaving I am about to teach you at this point is nothing like what you have learned so far. Although, it is as simples as up and down, up and down, but there is something unique to this so read carefully the instructions. Start weaving at the top, specifically on the upper right hand corner. Thread in the weft into a shuttle and begin weaving over and under, over and under and continue all the way around the loom, from front going to the back, then going to the front, and then going to the back. On and on this way it goes. When you reach near the end of the loom, around 1.5-

inches to the end, you can adjoin the warp thread ends you have pinned and weave it like one weft thread.

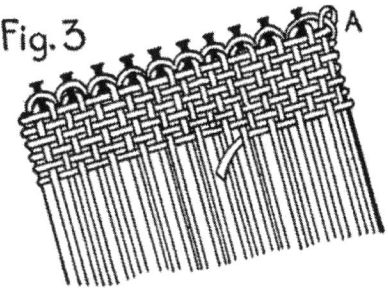

Fig. 3

4) If you need to finish or fasten ends of threads, sew them together.
5) When you have fully finished weaving the bag, you can now remove the pins. You can catch down top row of weft by stitching to warp. Then add a satin lining inside the bag and finish it with a zipper enclosure.

Wheels and Hoops as Looms

These circular items can be an embroidery hoop, bicycle rim, and even cartwheels can be drafted to serve as a weaving loom. In this section, I am going to teach you how to make circular rugs with the use of a 27-inch hula-hoop. The requirement for using wheels and hoops as looms is strength—you will know why as we go along the instructions.

Materials:
27-inch hula hoop
Strips of woolen cloth or cotton, cut straight or bias
4 strips of 31-inch long 3-4 inch wide cloth
Pins

Directions for use:

1) Readying your loom. So the first step in weaving with a hula hoop is to first wind a strip of cloth around the hoop. You can use the woolen cloth or strips of cotton to do this. You can refer to the figure below.

Fig. 1

2) Setting the warp thread. The next step is a bit hard and will need your strength. Now that

you have readied your 31 x 3 or 31 x 4 inch strips of cloth (make sure that you either stick to 3 or 4 inches and not mix and match 3 and 4 inch pieces of cloth). Now fold these strips to 1-inch width, making sure to keep the raw edges of the cloth inside. Stretch these trips across the hoop, and pin the edge of the cloth on the hoop. Create a total of 8 spokes and firmly sew the center where all the cloths meet. See figure below for a better visualization of this step.

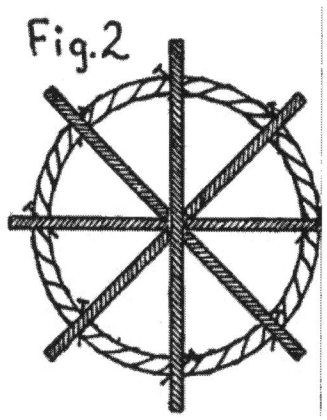

3) Weaving the weft. As you already know, for circular looms, you need an uneven number of spokes, since we have 8; we still need to add 1 spoke. How to do this? First ready your 3 or 4 inch cloth, fold it to an inch with the ragged

edges in. It also needs to be several yards long, so you can sew 2 to 3 strips together to make it long.

Begin by pinning this new strip right next to any spoke. Then bring the piece of cloth to the center of the circle, once in the middle, start to weave the piece of cloth up and down the spokes. Continue weaving until the center of your rug already has a diameter of at least 3-inches.

Fig.3

4) Once you have a 3-inch center diameter of woven cloth, start adding another strip. You can add this new strip right next to your added cloth and weave it going down. And once you reach the 3-inch center, reverse the movement of weaving and go back up such that you are forming a V. Then add another V-shaped weaving to each of the spoke sections, this will

then give you a total of 25 spokes. Ensure that when you add a new spoke, it must be in the opposite direction. For example, you are adding a new cloth and the weave pattern on the left started with an under, then the added cloth must be started as an over. Further, do not forget to pin the ends of the added cloths into the rim of the hula hoop. Continue the weaving process and sew in additional strips when needed. If the spokes are far apart, just weave in more cloth in a V formation in order to keep the cloths compact.

Fig.4

5) Once you have woven your rug completely, remove the pins that secure the warp and cloths. Fold them backwards and sew the loose ends in place. This is how a completed rug would look.

6) Pillow Top: With this technique, you can also make it as a pillow top, but of course this time you would be using better cloth options. A good decision would be to choose for colors that would match the room you intend to use the pillow on.
7) Doily: for doilies, I recommend using ¼-inch wide cloth for weft and warp. You can also explore other possibilities that you think may look good for your doily—the possibilities are endless you know!

Using the Weave-It Loom

Many of the processes that I have talked about above are do-it-yourself looms. However, there are looms that you can buy and one of them is the weave it loom. So how do you use a weave it loom?

1) Setting up the warp threads. Hold the weave-it with arrow 1 in front of you but pointing away from you. With the end of yarn toward you, hold it at arrow 1; draw the yarn in the middle of the pins on the far side of weave-it in direction of arrow 1. Move the yarn to the right, around the first two pins and then back to the side nearest you, drawing the yarn out between second and third pins at right of arrow 1. Tie securely to end of yarn close to pins. Pass yarn to right around next two pins and draw it to the far side, bringing it out between first and second pins in group directly across. Pass yarn to right around two pins and back to near side, out between first and second pins in next group, around two pins and back until you have reached curved arrow two. See figure below for a better visualization.

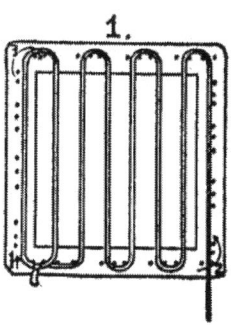

2) Turn loom so arrow 2 points away from you. Pass the yarn around the first two pins and go to the far side as you bring the yarn out in the middle of the first and second pins. Around two pins and back to near side between first and second pins in next group, repeating the process until you reach arrow three.

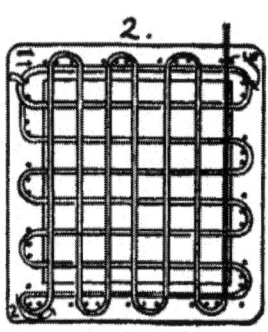

3) Turn loom so that arrow 3 points toward you. Pass the yarn through the first and second pins to the near side, coming out between first and second pins. Pass yarn around two pins and go back to far side as you bring the yarn out through the open space. Go around two pins and back to near side, coming out of the open space. Repeat this until the loom is filled.

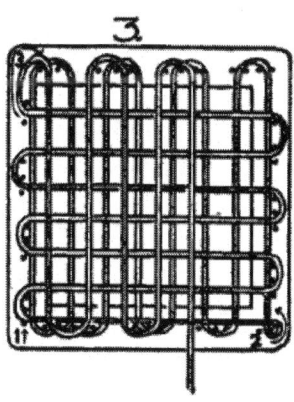

4) Weaving. Now you can begin weaving. You can measure your weft, by winding in loosely around the outside pins of the loom 4.5 times. Start at the W between the first and second pins, pass the threaded needle over outside loop, under next warp thread, over next, under, over, across and draw yarn through. Go around 2 pins and come back outside loop; go under, over, and so on—bringing the needle out at open space. Repeat the process, ending with the last row of weaving next to pins. Turn corner and tie yarn into first loop around pins.
5) To join the squares, stitch together using long thread left on square after weaving. When thread is almost used up, tie slip know or tack securely. Weave loose end of new thread 1-inch down on wrong side. At edge draw thread through two loops and tie a slip knot.

Fig.5

Conclusion

I hope you have learned a lot about weaving through this book. Once you have mastered making weave products, the next step is to graduate into a huge loom. When it comes to weaving, practice makes perfect. So, try to do small projects at a time, instead of one big project—because with smaller projects, you can see the results immediately and you will be tempted to make more. Once you get the satisfaction from seeing creations made by your own hand, that's the time to move on to bigger projects.

Copyright © 2015. All rights reserved.

Except as permitted under the United States Copyright Act of 1976, reproduction or utilization of this work in any form or by any electronic, mechanical, or other means, now known or hereafter invented, including xerography, photocopying, and recording, and in any information storage and retrieval system, is forbidden without written permission.

The ideas, concepts, and opinions expressed in this book are intended to be used for educational and reference purposes only. Author and publisher claim no responsibility to any person or entity for any liability, loss, or damage caused or alleged to be caused directly or indirectly as a result of the use, application, or interpretation of the material in this book.

Printed in Great Britain
by Amazon